Earth To Avni

Unravelling the curls

Avni Khandelwal

BookLeaf Publishing

India | USA | UK

Made with ❤ on the BookLeaf Publishing Platform
www.bookleafpub.in
www.bookleafpub.com

Dedication

*For the ones who feel too much, bend too far, and hope
too hard —*
your heart is not heavy — it's just full.

Preface

I've been scribbling on the backs of notebooks, the margins of registers and half-finished diaries for as long as I can remember. Writing has been a way to give the noises in my head and heart a home, and being the homebody I am, I've always turned to it for comfort.

Before I ever called myself a writer, I was a reader who found magic in dog-eared pages, the scent of a new book and characters that felt like they were speaking just to me. Somewhere between losing myself in those stories and living through my own, I found poetry, and over time, my poems became how I understood what I was feeling before I knew I was feeling it.

This book is made of twenty-one pieces of my heart, written across seasons of change.

Earth to Avni is the voice that pulls me back when growing up feels overwhelming.
It holds bittersweet nostalgia and goodbyes, people-pleasing and self-doubt, burnout and breakdowns, and the strange way we compare our insides to everyone else's outsides.

Unravelling the Curls is my way of untangling all that emotion, one poem at a time: messy, honest, and mine.

These poems aren't just about pain but the strength that comes from feeling it all. It's about showing up, even when you don't have the answers, and still finding the courage to keep going.

And when the weight feels unbearable, the last four poems in this book offer a shift. The poems allow you to step beyond yourself and into the world, linking adolescence's beautiful chaos to nature's quiet strength. Nature taught me what I couldn't learn: Change is a constant and breaking is simply part of becoming.

If you, like me, have ever thought that you're too sensitive, too emotional, too much — this is my love letter to you. Your feelings are not a weakness; they are the proof that you're alive, that you're feeling, and that you're trying. Writing this book is how I made peace with mine.

Welcome to my heart on paper. It holds pieces of the last fifteen years of my life. I hope, as you read, you find pieces of yourself too.
With love,
Avni Khandelwal

Acknowledgements

I dedicate this book to my biggest supporter, my fiercest critic, my therapist, my mother and my best friend: Nidhi Khandelwal- the quiet force behind every word I've ever written. She's the kind of woman who makes kindness powerful and turns any room into a home. The kind of woman who gives without expecting, loves without conditions, and somehow makes the impossible look effortless. She saw potential in me long before I ever knew what it looked like and has always believed in me, even when I didn't. She filled my world with stories of bold, brilliant women — from Palki Sharma to Lorelai Gilmore — never realising that the one I admired most was always her. If I grow into even half the woman she is, I'll have lived a life I'm proud of. She's not just the heart of our home — she's its foundation, its steady anchor, its soul. This book is as much yours as it is mine, Mumma. I am nothing without you.

An equally deserving dedication goes to my real-life superhero, my math critic, my father(or as I often call him, my "younger" brother): Ankur Khandelwal. He is easily the most kind-hearted, generous, and doting person I know. Since childhood, he has sown the seeds of my wild imagination through his painfully funny bedtime stories, which have now evolved into making up creative acronyms to memorise geography maps. He taught me never to settle for anything less than I deserved, to face every challenge with remarkable resilience (and a side of humour), and to never be afraid to stand up for myself. Thank you for being you, every single day.

I am proud, blessed and grateful to be able to call myself the daughter of the best people I know.

I am immensely grateful for my guiding pillars- my grandparents, Shiv Khandelwal, Pratima Khandelwal, Umesh Chandra Khandelwal and Saroj Khandelwal. Your love and blessings have shaped me into the person I am today. I carry your hopes, your dreams, and your lessons with me and hope to make you proud every step of the way. It is an honour to be your granddaughter.

Finally, to my younger self - thank you for feeling everything so deeply, even when the world made you think it was a flaw.
You are why I'm here.
You make me prouder every single day.
I hope, wherever you are in me, you are proud of me too.
I promise to take you with me wherever I go.

Every word and every experience has contributed to the words on these pages. To all those who have supported me, in ways big or small, I'm forever grateful. Thank you.

Ukiyo

I sit with a friend, my once verdant garden of felicity
uprooted,
I condemn, contemplate and cry my cries of misery
muted.
In my disguised bliss, I take out an orange and start to
peel,
It's not a habit, my spillage explains, for she's always
peeled them with a hue of zeal.

Her eyes: an evident concoction of concern, as she pulls
it away with love I can't dare ignore,
Deftly pulling out the sticky whites, feeds me one of
those little pieces she knows how much I adore.
"I hope you never learn to peel oranges Avni", a moment
worth all the friendship bracelets I never received,
Ghosts of my past fade; that slice of orange was all I
could ever need.

Aphelion

you changed. i did not.
apart; the sun and moon we are.
you lit the sky—alone.

Goodbyes

Watching myself ignore all the signs,
"The best friends with a telepathic mind."
But I sank deeper as we,
Separated into you and me.

A rubber band, stretched, nearly torn,
A silent tragedy, never fully born.
I overlooked your flaws while you hunted for mine,
Now I search for the good in a jagged goodbye.

No one told me how goodbyes would ache,
But we paused the bond before it could break.
Yet another friendship that slipped too fast,
All I ever wanted was for it to last.

Losing the laughter, the days we replayed,
As I watch you walk past that gate.
I'm letting you go, freeing the chain,
Because in my heart, I know we'll meet again.

Blue

She: a blue crayon, the one that quickly disappears,
Colouring the sky and oceans till there's nothing left of
her.
Overwatering plants; she doesn't know when to stop
giving,
Kills herself trying to be enough, in a world that doesn't
stop taking.

Indefinite pages of blue, she clenches her broken claws,
A delusional chase to become who she once was.
Desperate attempts to ignite a spark in her fire oh so
burntout,
Drowning expectations...unkept promises...an aimless
myriad of doubts.

A prevailing supernova; the death of yet another star,
A lost phoenix, with stars that now turn to bleeding
scars.
Yet each time the sky shows its wrath; a thunderous
brew,
It always comes back home to the Sun still the same
blue.

Nothing to Bury

i said your old name
just to taste the ash of it.
some deaths leave no graves.

Near yet Far

Flooded was my mind with the sanction of buried memories,
As I entered your once beloved cottage, shaped with love across centuries.
Your picture welcomed me, grandma, and grief settled in that frame,
How could you vanish, yet stay in every breath I claim?

The autumn leaves fell, crimson—your favourite season's hue,
I wish I'd saved each grocery list, each note, just to hold more of you.
Your scent, like something I'm losing day by day,
From secret stashes to tickle fights that couldn't stay.

I converse with you in silence, in rooms where your touch lingers,
But grief hides in quiet corners, slipping through my fingers.
Now I lay here in our Sunday spot, staring at the countless glinting stars,
The only difference is, I come alone, while you're six feet apart.

Wabi-sabi

Her soul is a kaleidoscope,
Bursting with colours...brimming with hope.
Reflecting hues; broken yet bold,
Shattering stories and healing scars; her eyes hold.

She constantly tries to be the best her,
When the "best" keeps getting better.
A delusional chase, she doesn't realise,
Her broken shards mould the beauty that lies.

A subtle shift, everything changes,
Perspective; one power...indefinite ranges.
A collection of shattered souls yearning peace,
United; from a mess to a masterpiece.

Sometimes the pieces fit, other times they do not,
Yet change is forever constant; a catalyst often forgot.
Comfortable being uncomfortable; key to weaving life's
loom,
For if a flower dare not change, how would it bloom?

Saudade

Love; a potent yet delicate feeling knowing no bounds,
Bridging indefinite gaps in the labyrinth of life.
The garth of our hearts, it beautifully surrounds,
Healing the butterflies that succumbed and died.

The way the moon dies each night to let the sun breathe,
The way nature never knows when to stop giving,
Each leaf that falls only to rise, new life beneath,
Love is never the end to something; just the beginning.

The blood rushing into rosy cheeks,
The silence speaking for each doting emotion.
The language of raw feelings; love bespeaks,
Unconditional love—drowning in devotion.

From once upon a time to happily ever afters,
Love writes itself in ink and silent chapters.

Unanchored

a relentless tide.
with no moon to call it back.
and I stay unheard.

Scripted

i stitched wounds in verse.
i bled behind the curtain.
still, they clapped on cue.

Eraya: fortune's favourite

Gifted, talented, special: common words that once felt
like home,
Proud reflections in a plethora of trophies; alluring and
chrome,
"An example for others"..."A pleasure to have in class."
Looking out of a window that now lies as shattered
pieces of glass.

Delusional, desperate, disheartened: she tries yet again,
Straight A's and a doting smile: a short-lived reign.
A labyrinth, with each turn leading back to the start,
An everlasting game; the one functioning button is
'restart'.

She knows that burning out is how a star is born,
Weaving together the pieces of her past, ripped and torn.
New beginnings make destinations closer, not far,
For there are days when the Sun believes it is just a star.

Fairest to Lose

mirror on the wall—
you crowned me easiest unloved.
I wore it like truth.

The Red Rose

She walked in the dusk with a shattered heart,
A subtle scarlet hint glinting; a state of art.
Her acid tears sizzling on the numbing snow,
Looking up to see a faint crimson silhouette, growing
like a willow.

A paragon red rose: she saw,
Its valiant aura leaving her in awe.
Pondering how if a petty wispy flower could grow in the
unmerciful cold,
How much power has she let the meaningless words of
others hold?

She craved for flowers to bloom the same way,
From the labyrinths within the core of her broken heart,
someday
And then the petals bloomed, leaves grew, thorns
pricked: she arose,
The story of how one day Avni became the red rose.

To Be, Then Not Be

i craved to be you,
but I'm nothing but your shadow.
now I don't know who I'm not.

To Be, Then Not Be

Hearthless

never learnt to say no.
grief is love without a home.
so I keep it warm.

Ouroboros

Rewatch, repeat, reload: my ouroboros,
The poet in me refusing to write prose.
A phoenix reborn: only to be the same,
The fireball and luna dance; an eternal game.

The candles are starting to crowd the cake,
My ghosts mourn yet another acerbic wake.
The flames of change dance around me,
A flicker that whispers but never sets me free.

I surrender to the fire; broken and outworn,
But ash only sleeps before it's reborn.

Eulogy

they buried my name
in snow they called coincidence.
the snow never melts.

A Monsoon Serenade

The harmony of the rhythmic pitter-patter,
The chorus of quintessential raindrops as they scatter.
The monsoon arrives - a boon from above.
Quenching the earth with boundless love.

As each raindrop kisses the soil, igniting life,
The land awakens adorned in shades, so green and
divine.
The scent of heavenly petrichor hung in the air,
Lighting up hearts, exiling despair.

The subtle psithurism of the crimson leaves,
The overwhelming elation a pluviophile receives.
The musty bark smell: an intoxicating perfume,
Like a celestial song, the evergreen magic of monsoon.

Within the Monsoon's solace, our souls unite,
A cosmic bond with nature, restoring our inner light.
How beautiful the story of monsoon; onerous and
intense,
A sole raindrop making its way through the heavens
only to rise again.

Reflections: Of Atoms and Ashes

Mother Earth; a mystery laced in veiled riddles,
We've anchored her pulse in uncertain middles.
Every atom within our restless minds still spins,
Dancing in silver shoes, from mitosis to sins.

Humans; the emblem of excess and greed,
Planting decay where there once bloomed seed.
Yet even now, as machines rise and grow,
We bow our heads - and call it progress below.

She, the Earth, who once taught us grace,
Now bears the burden of every trace.
We mistook her silence for mercy, sublime,
And left her with wounds no clock can rewind.

Endless Endeavours

Carrying happiness, love, wisdom in its warm embrace,
The brook's mellifluous symphony; a bewitching trance.
Glints in the golden farewell...murmurs in the moon's solace,
As it slithers through the labyrinth of its indefinite expanse.

With the brawn of Poseidon, it roars and reminisces,
The ability to endure what may come its way.
Flooding vacant tear ducts. burning the snow's bridges,
Establishing its ascendancy in each array.

Life, like this river, cascades and flows,
The constant clockwork, we forever chase after.
Yet the veiled secrets of time, only the river knows,
The reins of water encompassing every chapter.

Nature's Trance

Mother Earth; boundless euphoria in its embrace,
The mellifluous symphony of nature; a mystic solace.
Witnessing the aurora and the luna's dance,
The paragon nature pulls me into its trance.

The flowers blush in fading hues of pink,
The crimson sky kisses the mountain's brink.
A story of colours, diversity and romance,
The paragon nature pulls me into its trance.

Verdant serenity all around; truly one of a kind,
Melodious nature forever echoes in my mind.
Drifting through the labyrinth of vast expanse,
The paragon nature pulls me into its trance.

The breeze - the epitome of tranquillity.
The trees reply with timeless humility.
The lavender haze enraptures my heart with a glance,
The paragon nature pulls me into its trance.

The murky mist; the beauty of the unknown,
The wildflowers teaching me how to heal alone.
Sunsets mean giving yourself one more chance,
The paragon nature pulls me into its trance.

9 789370 927971